THE MAGIC STORYSINGER

THE MAGIC STORYSINGER

FROM THE FINNISH EPIC TALE *KALEVALA*
RETOLD AND ILLUSTRATED BY M.E.A. McNEIL

Stemmer House
PUBLISHERS, INC.
OWINGS MILLS, MARYLAND

Inquiries should be directed to
Stemmer House Publishers, Inc.
2627 Caves Road
Owings Mills, Maryland 21117

A *Barbara Holdridge* book

Printed and bound in Hong Kong

First edition

Library of Congress Cataloging-in-Publication Data

McNeil, M. E. A.
　　The magic storysinger : a tale from the Finnish epic Kalevala /
retold and illustrated by M.E.A. McNeil.
　　　　p.　　cm.
　　"A Barbara Holdridge book"—T.p. verso.
　　Summary : From his mysterious birth as the old-man son of the air
maiden through his various adventures and accomplishments, Finnish
folk hero Väinämöinen makes use of his ability to create magic songs
and spells.
　　ISBN 0-88045-128-9 (hardbound) : $16.95
　　[1. Folklore—Finland.]　I. Kalevala.　II. Title.　III. Title :
Magic story singer.
PZ8.1.M466Mag　1993
[398.21]—dc20　　　　　　　　　　　　　　　　93-27467
　　　　　　　　　　　　　　　　　　　　　　　CIP
　　　　　　　　　　　　　　　　　　　　　　　AC

For
Ellen Meljia Leivo McNeil
and
Jerome C. Draper

CONTENTS

1 The Birth of the Storysinger   12

2 The Mermaids' Oak   18

3 How Väinö Discovered his Magic   22

4 The Battle of the Storysingers   26

5 Aino's Escape   34

6 Väinö's Bride Slips Off His Hook   39

7 Jouka's Revenge   42

8 Louhi of North Farm   46

9 Louhi's Daughter   51

10 The Healer   54

11 The Sampo   60

12 Death's Island   65

13 In the Belly of the Giant   70

14 The Race   77

15 Plowing Snakes   84

16 The Sea Battle for the Sampo   92

17 How Louhi Brought Winter to Finland   99

18 Väinämöinen's Promise   106

ILLUSTRATIONS

"Ilmatar plunged down to the bottom of the sea." Frontispiece

*"Out of the sea walked a man the size
of Väinö's thumb."*   18–19

"Cuckoo, sing a celebration!"   25

"In a moment, the sleighs crashed."   28–29

*"Aino opened the trunk within the trunk and
the box within the box."*   37

*"All winter Väinö fished, but he did not catch
his bride."*   40–41

"The arrow missed Väinö and hit his flying stallion."   44–45

"That is a man; the wind does not complain so much."   49

*"The maiden of North Farm sat on the rim of
a rainbow."*   53

"Bring a drop of honey to seal this sweet promise."   56

"Ilmarinen flew on a whirling, swirling journey."   62

*"Death's daughter was washing black clothes in
the black water."*   67

"Out climbed Väinö over the brambly maw."   74

*"She saw a great ship racing against a stallion
pulling a sleigh."*   80–81

"One song after another flowed from the storysinger."   88–89

"Their boat stopped dead in the water."   94

"Never had they felt such joy."   100–101

*"Louhi sent the fierce, long, freezing
Northland Winter."*   104–105

*"He strode out into the winter cold, keeping the child next
to his heart."*   109

THE MAGIC STORYSINGER

1
THE BIRTH OF THE STORYSINGER

WHEN VÄINÖ WAS BORN, he was an old man. So he did not spend time growing up thinking about what he was going to be. It happened that he became a magic storysinger—perhaps by accident, and perhaps because he was born to it.

It began with his mother, Ilmatar, the daughter of Air. For ages there was nothing for her to do but float in the dark and lonely heavens. There was nothing but a swirl of seeds—the seeds of all stories.

"Ooooooooooo!" she called out into the void. It surprised her when her voice stopped somewhere below, for the sound usually went on endlessly.

"Good," she thought. "Something else." She dropped a shoulder, sending her cloudy body down toward the other.

What she saw was the most wonderful thing that she had ever seen, since she had never before seen anything at all. There below her stretched the glassy, calm sea. In it was her reflection.

A sudden wind swept the air maiden into the water, tumbled her in the waves, and soaked the story seeds with sea foam. By the time the gale passed, young Väinö had sprouted from the seeds and curled up in her belly.

The air maiden was too heavy to rise out of the water. She swam eastward and westward. She swam south and northwestward. Time passed, and Väinö grew older within her. As she swam, she could not tell the salt of her tears from the salt of the ocean.

"It was better to be a maiden of the air than a mother of the water," she cried.

A duck appeared—fluttering about, looking for a place to land. "I can't build my nest on the wind," she honked. "I can't build it on the waves."

The maiden knew well how it felt to be homeless, so she raised her knee above the surface of the water to give the duck a resting place. This was a good arrangement until the bird built her nest there and laid seven eggs—six of gold and the seventh of iron. Then she sat herself down to brood on them. The maiden's knee became warmer and warmer until it felt as though her skin had begun to smolder. She stayed still as long as she could. All at once, her knee jerked and the eggs went flying.

They shattered into beautiful things:

the top half of one into the dome of the sky
the lower half of another into the earth below
a yolk became the sun
a white became the moon and
spotted pieces became stars in the sky.

All the pieces kept moving. The sun and moon and earth moved into a cycle of day and night. Day and night turned in the greater cycle of the months and the moon grew brighter and smaller. The months spun into an even greater cycle of seasons. The days and the months repeated themselves for years. Round and round the patterns turned. The maiden watched the winter sun grow dimmer. She watched the summer sun return. Still she swam the open sea, hopelessly wandering.

One morning, Ilmatar lifted her head up above the vast ocean, and then she plunged down, down to the bottom of the sea. She touched the bottom with her foot and hollowed out a deep trough for sea creatures. She formed islands and hidden reefs. She moved her hand and pushed the headlands up. She nestled her back against the land and formed the shore, hollowing out inlets for the fish with her feet. With the back of her head she shaped the bays of Finland in the place called Kaleva. Then she began to paint—some say to write. She marbled patterns onto rocks, cut signs into crags, drew lines onto cliffs.

When she finished, Väinö had grown old. It was cramped and dark where he was. All the ruckus with the eggs had made him curious about the sun and the moon. So he called to them to help him. "Moon, free me!" he shouted. "Sun, let me out!"

Then he waited. The moon did not arrive. The sun did not come. They silently traced their cycles within cycles over the vast sea.

"If no one will help me, I'll have to help myself," said Väinö. He turned the lock with his toe, slid the bolt with his finger, crawled through the door, and with his knees he pushed himself headlong into the ocean.

He tumbled to the surface. There was nothing but the sea. He floated there as the sun and the moon circled, as the moon waxed and waned, as the seasons came. At last, Väinö washed ashore at Kaleva. He pulled himself out of the water and stood in wonder at the curved bay and the patterns on the craggy rocks.

This was the birth of Väinämöinen. This also was the birth of *sisu*—a special courage of the Finnish people to do things for themselves. Some say it is born of long waiting in the dark.

2
THE MERMAIDS' OAK

UP JUMPED VÄINÖ and had a good look around the place. It was all rock and earth. Nothing grew anywhere. He put his head in his hands and said, "What can be done in this impossible place?"

When he looked up, a knee-high gnome stood before him—Sampsa the field spirit. With a grin, the gnome began to sow seeds across the land. He tossed them everywhere—across rich soil, swamps, stony fields, hills and along the edges of lakes and streams. As soon as the seeds touched the ground, trees began to grow. The field spirit hopped over sprouting saplings and clumps of pines spreading their needled branches. A handful of

seeds over his shoulder became a stand of fir on a knoll, a toss on a breeze became alders in loose loam, and a dance along a riverbank left willows and sallows and rowans where they could keep their feet wet.

The acorns that rolled near the mermaids' rocks were sprouted by mermaid love songs. One oak tree stretched its branches up above the other trees. It grew until it stopped the drifting clouds. It kept growing until it blocked the light of the sun and moon.

"Magic is so unpredictable," mused Sampsa.

"A day without the sun and moon is a day without joy," said Väinö. "Who can fell this tree and bring back the light?" Sampsa shrugged his shoulders. He was a forest gnome and wouldn't dream of cutting a tree.

Out of the sea walked a man the size of Väinö's

thumb. He was armored in copper from his helmet to his tiny boots. In his copper glove he held a copper ax. "I have come to fell the great oak tree," said the little man.

"This is not what I had in mind," said Väinö.

But as he spoke, the little sea spirit stamped his foot on the ground, grew huge, spit in his hands and went to work. With his ax he struck the tree so hard that a chunk of metal flew off the ax and landed on the beach. The second blow was so fierce that fire flashed from his blade. His third blow shattered the trunk and chips flew in every direction. The fall of the enormous tree sounded like thunder. Pieces flew across the water, and there they rocked about and began journeys, like little boats, carrying the mermaids' magic. Then the man, once more as tiny as he had come, walked back into the water. In the first lap of a wave, he disappeared.

Väinö did not pick up a piece of the oak, which might have been useful. Someone else did pick up a branch, and it may not have served her well.

Pieces of the magic tree drifted windward to Pohjola in the far cold North. There, on the tip of a long headland, the daughter of Louhi, the mistress of North Farm, was washing her weavings on the rocks. She found an oak branch bobbing toward shore, put it with her laundry in her birch rucksack, and skiied home to show her mother.

Louhi wondered at the oak branch. She turned it over in her leathery hands. She put on her skis and made her way to her secret vault on Copper Mountain, where she dug away the snow and frozen earth. Beneath lay a layer of scree—bits of rock ground off when an ancient glacier moved its slow course from Pohjola all the way to Kaleva and melted into the ocean. Beneath the gravel lay solid, cold granite. Within the granite lay Louhi's vault. Within the vault were nine locked copper doors. Inside she planted the oak that the mermaids filled with love magic. Perhaps that was why many suitors came to court her daughter. The oak did not grow in the frozen earth as Louhi had hoped, and all the suitors were left with broken hearts.

3
HOW VÄINÖ DISCOVERED HIS MAGIC

WHEN THE GREAT OAK had fallen and the sun and moon shone again, the earth came back to life. The heaths were covered with heather and the dells with bird cherries.

There were wild herbs and berries and nuts to gather, and even animals to hunt. But there were no grains to eat. Väinö pondered this problem as he wandered to the shore. There, in the fine sand, he found a barley seed. He got down on his knees and discovered more barley seeds. He gathered them carefully in a weasel paw pouch.

He set out into the forest to plant the seeds. As he began, a cuckoo called out to him.

"Stop! I have some good advice. Don't throw your grain seeds here in the woods. Clear land so that your crop can have light."

"That makes sense," said Väinö. So he set about making an ax out of the sharp metal shard which had flown off the little man's ax. He fastened it to a pine-branch handle with twisted birch twigs. With this ax, he began to cut down the trees.

Chopping down a tree was a big job for an old man, and hatcheting a whole field was more than Väinö could do. Still, he hacked at it. His back and his shoulders ached. When he came to the little birch tree where the cuckoo sat, he stopped and leaned on his ax. "Well, my friend, if I leave you your tree, it's one less that I have to cut."

The clearing was no bigger than a path around the cuckoo's tree—hardly enough for a field. Poor old Väinö sat down on a rock too tired to move.

An eagle, circling overhead, landed in the tree and asked, "Why have you saved this little birch tree in the middle of your work?"

"I have saved it for the birds," said Väinö.

"You did very well," said the eagle. "For your generosity, I shall offer you some help."

The eagle dove at the rock where the old man sat and struck its beak against the granite. A spark jumped up and so did Väinö. The North wind whipped the spark into a flame, and fire burned furiously until it made a clearing.

Out of his pouch, Väinö took his barley seeds. As he sowed he sang:

With my back bent I sow barley
On land formed by my mother's hand.
Earth, push the seeds up from the ashes,
Let a thousand seedlings pop up
And on each one a hundred branches
For the trouble I have taken.

Ukko, Father of the Heavens,
Gather clouds from all directions,
Knock them all together headlong,
Dropping water from the sky.
Drip down honey from the heavens,
To grow barley for my bread.

As it happened, a cloud bank had been rising up from the West, and another from the South. When they flowed together, water rained from the sky. The barley grew well, and soon it was three joints high, covered with six-sided ears of grain. The cuckoo sat singing in the little birch tree in the middle of the grain field.

"Look what I have sung up!" he said. "I must be a magic singer! Cuckoo, sing a celebration!"

Now the grain grew in its own time, and the cuckoo sang whenever she pleased. But at that moment, the cukoo was in the mood to sing, and Väinö chuckled with joy at his wonderful power.

4
THE BATTLE OF THE STORYSINGERS

VÄINÖ WAS CONVINCED that he must be a great storysinger, and, as often happens, what he thought was true about himself became true over time. Day after day he gathered songs and practiced his craft. He sang of how things began and of ancient wisdom that is no longer understood. He discovered magic songs that could create things, and, to his wonder, he sang up a bow, a boat, a horse, a sleigh.

The news of Väinö's singing spread quickly from Pohjola to Lapland. A thin young Lapp named Joukahainen liked to think of himself as a storysinger. He was wandering about when he heard about the great man in Kaleva. He decided to challenge Väinö to a singing match.

"He can bewitch you," warned his father.

"He will sing you right into the snow," said his mother.

"Father, you know something. Mother, you know perhaps a little more," answered Jouka. "But I know the most. I'll sing the singer into stone shoes, with a boulder for his hat."

He took out the family sleigh, hitched up the best horse and rode away. Helter-skelter he drove, cracking his whip all day, another day and then a third—until he reached Kaleva.

Väinö was riding in his sleigh along the road, when he saw Jouka heading straight at him from the opposite direction. In a moment, the two crashed—sleigh shafts caught, traces knotted, harnesses twined, sleighs overturned. Väinö untangled himself from his lap robe, crawled out of his sleigh, brushed the snow off his beard and said, "Whose reckless young one are you, cracking my sleigh into kindling?"

"I am Joukahainen. Who are you, pitiful old man?"

"I am Väinämöinen the storysinger. Move aside a little now so I may pass, since I am much older than you."

"Ha!" said Jouka. "Age counts for nothing. It's how smart a man is that matters. He who has the greater knowledge will hold the road and the other move aside. Let us sing our magic until one wins the game. If you are the famous singer, let's begin our contest now, and you will start reciting."

"What do I know?" said Väinö. "I have spent my days here singing with the cuckoo. Since you seem to know so much, tell me all about it."

"Well, I know a thing or two!" shouted Jouka, and he began his song:

A smoke hole must be in the roof,
And the flame set in the fire space.
Northland plowing is with reindeer,
The Southland plow beast is a mare,
Lapland harnesses elk for plowing,
And I can even tell you more.
Sea life is pleasant for a seal . . .

"Child's chatter!" bellowed Väinö. "Tell me about how things began. Of things no one else knows."

Jouka's face reddened. He sang louder:

The cuckoo is a bird, I'm sure.
I say the viper is a snake.
Maybe willow was the first tree.
Hot water hurts; a burn is bad . . .

"Not as bad as this song," said Väinö. "That's enough."

"Wait. I remember more. I remember plowing the sea bed, pushing up the earth to make hills and mountains . . . "

"Do tell," said Väinö.

Jouka put one hand on his chest, raised the other to the sky and sang on:

I was sixth of seven heroes,
Present at the earth's creation,
Raising up the sky's great pillars,
Guiding moon and sun in orbit,
Scattering the stars in pictures . . .

"Liar!" bellowed Väinö, furiously. "I know who was present at the earth's creation, who flung the moon and sun into orbit, who scattered the stars, and I know, my boy, that she did not see you there."

"If you do not respect the power of my wisdom, I shall have to prove myself with my sword," challenged Jouka, drawing his blade and thrusting it at Väinö.

"Well, neither your foolish wit nor your pin of a sword scare me enough to bother with fighting," said Väinö.

Jouka twisted his hair. "If you will not stand and fight, I'll sing a spell that will turn you into a pig!"

"Enough!" Väinö's deep voice answered like a tidal wave. The echo rocked lakes; cliffs cracked.

Väinö the storysinger sang out, his spells filling the air: the young man's bow sprouted leaves, his whip turned into a shore reed, his fine horse became a rock, his sword streaked across the sky as lightning, and his feathered arrows turned into flying hawks. He turned Jouka's cap into a cloud and his gloves into lily pads. Then he enchanted the boy into marsh mud up to his knees.

Jouka tried to lift his foot. He could not move.

Väinämöinen, story singer,
Wisest teller, greatest knower,
Magic spinner of the ages:
Undo your charm from a poor boy,
Whose parents mourn on Lapland's shore.

"You're getting better," said Väinö, but he did nothing.

"I will pay a ransom for my freedom. You may have one of my two fine bows," said Jouka.

"I have no need of your bow. I have conjured bows for every peg in my house," answered the storysinger. Then he sang the young man into the mud up to his thighs.

"I have two boats; one is light and fast and one is wide for carrying things. You may have either one," cried out the Lapp.

"I don't need your boat. I have sung boat spells until I have boats rolled up on logs in every cove," said Väinö, who then sang the lad up to his chin in swamp moss and slime.

Desperately Jouka called out, "I know what you do not have! What you cannot make with your magic! Give me back my life, and I shall give you my sister Aino as your wife. She could bring you a child."

"A child," said Väinö quietly, and he sat down on a rock. "Yes, a child!" he cried out in delight. "I would like to have a child." Then he began to sing his songs backward. Jouka emerged out of the slime, the horse whinnied, the whip and sleigh were ready to go.

Jouka wasted no time leaving, but his ride home was

not happy. He thought only of how he had to tell his parents that he had pledged his sister away.

To Jouka's surprise, his mother was overjoyed. She clapped her hands and rubbed them together.

"What an honor to have the famous storysinger in our family! I have always wanted to have a great man as kin."

But his sister Aino wept the day she heard the news. And she wept the day after as well.

"What do you have to cry for? You could not find a greater man," said her mother.

"I cry because my long braids which fly free will be bound up tight under a wife's kerchief."

"Silly girl," replied her mother.

"We shall see," whispered Aino under her breath.

5
AINO'S ESCAPE

AINO WAS WALKING through the woods gathering birch twigs to make sauna whisks for her father, her mother and her troublesome brother. Väinö found her and hurried after her. But he did not know what to do. He had no idea how to talk to her, what words to say, what way to win her. He was a mighty magician, but he had never had a friend, a playmate, and he had learned none of the little lessons of childhood.

"My prize!" shouted Väinö. "All mine! The beads around your neck are for no one else but me. The ribbons in your hair are for no one else but me. Your little finger rings are for no one else but me."

"Not for you nor for anyone else," answered Aino. She tore off her trinkets and threw them to the ground. She ran home in tears.

Aino's father sat by the gate carving an ax handle for his new son-in-law. "Why are you crying?" he asked.

"I have good reason to cry. I no longer have my beads or my ring or the red ribbon from my hair," she answered.

Her brother was sitting in the doorway, whittling arrows with sharp tips. "Why are you crying?" he asked.

"I have good reason to weep. I no longer have my ornaments or my silk hair ribbon."

Her mother was skimming cream by the inglenook. "Why are you crying?" she asked.

"There is good reason for my grief. I was coming home from gathering sauna branches, and the Kalevalander met me in the woods. He said I could not wear my shiny things for anyone else but him. I threw down the colored threads from my hair and the jewelry from my body and left them for the earth to take."

"Now, now," said Aino's mother. "You worry so! You are going to marry a great man who will feed you plenty of butter with pork and sweet crumbcakes to make you plump and pretty. Now run along and find your wedding clothes. Go to the storehouse on the hill where they are hidden. There you will see a chest. Within it there is another chest and in that there is a box within a box, with a lid of many colors. Open it and you will find six gold sun-forged belts and seven blue moon-spun dresses."

Aino ran outside in despair. "The bridal clothes are a sorry bargain for a lifetime of weeping in the house of a stranger. I know the rules for a wife: She must bow down and be pleasant, ask when to come and when to go. She must get up before the sun to build the fire just the way the master wants it, sweep the wide floor, wash the long board table, carry the water buckets, grind, sift, stack, wash, spin and stoke the sauna for him. She is a prisoner tied up in a flaxen scarf, working after the horses are exhausted—all the while at his beckoning. And will he peel a birch whip to keep it that way, as husbands can do?

"Once I was lucky—dancing on pathways, singing over the hills, playing games among the trees. Now I am unlucky—dark as the still water at the bottom of a well. Like crusted snow at the foot of a ridge.

"It is better not to be born than to leave behind my songs and dreams. If I had died at six days, I would have taken no more than a handspan of linen, some tears from my mother, a few from my father, and none at all from my brother. Better to be a sister to the fish than a bond slave to a husband."

She walked, weeping, up to the storehouse, opened the trunk inside the trunk and the box within the box and lifted the colored lid. She slipped the moon-spun dresses over her head and fastened the long skirts with the precious belts. She put gold ornaments across her forehead and silver ones in her hair. In silken stockings and fine shoes, she tramped to the stream and followed its reed-grown bank down to the sea. There, at the end of a headland, the mermaids were bathing.

Aino threw the dresses on a willow, the stockings on an aspen, the shoes on a rock and the ornaments in the

sand. The mermaids beckoned her. She splashed along the shore and, with them, she dove into the depths of the sea.

6
VÄINÖ'S BRIDE SLIPS OFF HIS HOOK

VÄINÖ SOON LEARNED that his prize had swum off with the mermaids. But he did not give up so easily. He paddled his boat out to the tip of the headland where the mermaids play. There he fished for many mornings, casting out his line and dipping back and forth with his hand net. He angled and dangled until his copper fishing rod quivered and the bright line straightened. A bite! He pulled up a huge fish and dropped it into his boat.

"That's a fishy-looking fish," said Väinö, as he poked it and flipped it over. "Hmm, too smooth for a whitefish, too light for a salmon, and look—no fins!"

Väinö grabbed the hilt of his knife and drew it back to gut the fish, shouting, "Breakfast, lunch and dinner!" Just as quickly, the fish flipped over the side of the boat into the sea.

Then it raised its head and its smooth right shoulder and spoke. "You, Väinämöinen, don't know a fish from a true love. I could have been your mate, to stay forever, to be warmed by your arms, to bring fire into our house, to share our meals. I was not a prize to be won in a contest. I was a maid, Jouka's sister Aino, and you, the smart one, were a fool."

"Oh, Aino," cried Väinö. "Come back!" But she did not come back again, ever. He trolled with his nets across

the gulf and then along the sound, around the islands and all along the shore of Lapland, singing sadly,

Careless Väinö, without knowing,
Won a game and lost what matters.

All winter he fished, but he did not catch his bride.

7
JOUKA'S REVENGE

VÄINÖ'S GRIEF WAS SO GREAT that the cuckoos in Kaleva stopped singing. "Mother," he cried out to the sky, "help me, for my heart is broken."

Ilmatar, spirit of the air, whispered on the wind, "Forget the Lapp girl. I saw a maiden in Pohjola at North Farm more beautiful and nimble than any I have seen in all my wanderings."

Old Väinö got himself up. He decided to travel north to have a look. He saddled his straw-colored horse, put the bit in its mouth, the bridle over its head and himself on its back. He rode to the sea and out over the water without a hoof splashing—along the coast of Lapland on his way to the far North.

There the young Lapp Jouka waited for his revenge. It was all he had thought of since the storysinger sang him down. He had made a new bow of iron. He had dipped his arrow points in snake venom.

Jouka fished near his farmhouse at a stream which fed into the sea. He tied a deer-hair fly on his line. The trout paid no attention because a new hatch of small, dark stone flies flitted across the rushing surface, where the ice had washed away. But Jouka did not care that the fish would not bite—even on his fly made of muskrat hair or his bear-hair fly. He was after a bigger prize. One morning among many, Jouka stood knee-deep in the stream, scanning the sky. He saw what looked like a cloud over the ocean. It was Väinö on his straw-gold horse on his way to Pohjola. Jouka drew his bow.

"Where are you pointing that bow?" called his mother.

"I am aiming at the heart of Väinämöinen," answered Jouka.

"Stop!" she cried. "If the storysinger were to fall, so would his songs. All joy would vanish, for there is no singing in Tuonela, the land of the dead."

For a moment Jouka wavered, one hand holding firmly "yes" and the other pulling strongly "no." Then he made his choice and told her, "Let the joy go with the songs. I will kill him and I'm ready." He chose the swiftest arrow in his quiver, laid the groove against the bowstring and drew it back. He raised the bow to his right shoulder and sighted Väinö along the arrow. But his mother's question moved his finger, pulling the bow ever so slightly, bending the arrow's journey until it just missed Väinämöinen and hit his flying stallion. It hit above the right front foreleg and knocked him from the sky to drown. Down went Väinö into the water.

"You won't sing me down again, Väinämöinen!" shouted the young Lapp. "What's left of you will sink in the sea, and I am done."

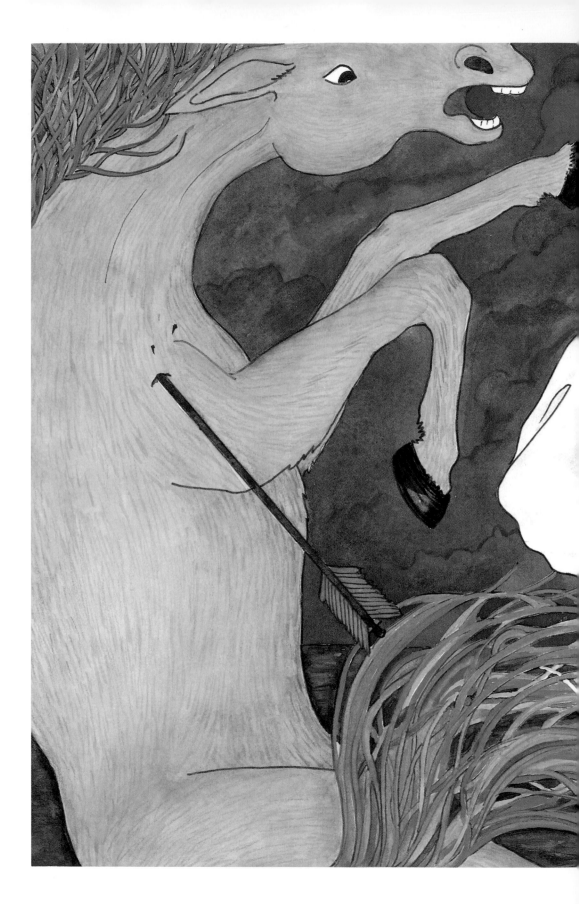

8
LOUHI OF NORTH FARM

BECAUSE VÄINÖ WAS BORN IN THE SEA, he did not drown. But swim as he might, he was washed one way and drifted another until he was far out from shore.

"Here I am, floating like a ball in a game between the wind and the tide. I'm shivering with cold, and my fingers are white and puckered like old fruit."

As it happened, the eagle was flying over and saw Väinö bobbing in the water. "What are you doing down there?"

"I set out to find a wife at North Farm. Joukahainen the Lapp shot my horse from under me. I fell into the water and have been swimming against the waves ever since. I don't know whether I will sink from tiredness or from hunger first.

"Hop on and I'll give you a ride," said the eagle. Väinö pulled himself up by the wing of the bird and straddled his back. The eagle soared on the path of Ahava, the cold spring wind, to the farthest northern land. The sky grew darker and the cold became bitter. When they arrived at Pohjola, the eagle dropped Väinö on the shore at the mouth of the river which led to North Farm. Then he flew away. Väinö, wet and shaking, his beard tangled with seaweed, huddled on the dark shore and wept.

Louhi, the mistress of North Farm, had long been at her tasks before her spotted dog began to bark. She heard a moaning from the direction of the sea. "That is a man. The wind does not complain so much."

She pushed her rowboat into the river and soon found Väinö shivering on the shore. "Ho, you miserable old codger, you really are in a strange land."

"That I know," said Väinö.

"What sort of man are you?" asked Louhi.

"Once I was the famous storysinger Väinämöinen. Now I don't even know myself."

Louhi understood that here was a valuable prize washed up on her shore. She helped him into her boat, sat him in the stern, settled into the oars, and rowed the whimpering old man back upstream to North Farm. There she fed him, warmed him in her sauna and rubbed him dry.

"Now how was it that I found you weeping and wailing on my shore?"

"I have reason to weep, said Väinö. "I was dropped into the endless sea and now I am dropped onto this tree-less waste, where nothing but the wind is familiar."

"Don't whine, Väinämöinen. Stay and enjoy life; here you will feast on salmon," said Louhi.

"Water from a birch bark shoe at home is better than honey wine from a golden bowl among strangers. All I want is to go back to Kaleva," said Väinö.

"So what will you give me," said Louhi, "if I send you home?"

"Whatever you ask," he answered. "To hear the cuckoo again, I shall give you a tall hat full of gold and silver coins."

"Now, Väinö, I am not asking for playthings. What I want is for you to make me a mill—a sampo—to grind out a harvest of all good things for North Farm. You can make it out of this barleycorn."

"Only the blacksmith Ilmarinen could forge such a thing," said Väinö. "If you will send me home, I promise I shall send him to you to hammer out your sampo."

"The one who makes the sampo shall have my daughter as his reward," said Louhi. She hitched a rein-deer to her sleigh and sat the storysinger in it. As she put the reins in his hands, she warned, "Do not raise your head to look up or a sad day will come to you."

Then Väinämöinen urged the animal to a run and

headed straight for Kaleva without looking back. It might have been better for him if he had remembered not to look up.

9
LOUHI'S DAUGHTER

THE MAIDEN OF NORTH FARM sat on the rim of a rainbow, working at a loom. She was weaving with threads from the colors of the prism. The shuttle hummed as she wove.

Väinämöinen was bumping along toward home when he heard the sound of the loom high above his head. He looked up. There she was, dressed in white, weaving on a brilliant rainbow in the sky. He stopped his horse at once and called to her, "Come, step down into my sleigh!"

"Why should a maiden get into your sleigh?" she asked.

"Ah, to bake my honey bread in Kaleva!"

"I have heard the birds singing, and the words they sing are these," she said.

Bright are the days of summer time,
But brighter still a maiden's life.
Cold is iron in a cold spell,
Colder is life as a daughter-in-law.

"Bird-chirping! A daughter is only a child until she is married! Now I am quite a remarkable man," said Väinö.

"I would think of you as remarkable if you could split a hair in two," said the maiden, as she began weaving again.

Väinö pulled a white hair out of his beard. He sang a charm as his knife pared two fine strands from one. "There you have them. Let's go!"

"Not till I see you tie a knot in an egg," she replied, as her shuttle whizzed back and forth.

Väinö hummed a charm. He plucked an egg from the nest of a bird who squawked and scolded as he tied a knot in it. "That's that. Let's be off!"

But the maiden would not come down into his sleigh. Instead, she tossed down her spindle. "I might marry you if you could build, from my distaff, a boat that could launch itself."

"No one can match me as a boat builder," boasted Väinö. He began to chop and fashion a boat, singing about his skill. His bravado came to an abrupt stop when the ax-blade lurched and the sharp iron edge sank into his knee.

"Ayeeee, ax! My leg is no tree!" cried Väinö. He tore lichens and moss from the rocks to make a poultice, but the bleeding did not stop. He recited all the magic words he knew, but he could not staunch the flow. He threw himself into the sleigh, weeping with pain, flicked the whip over the reindeer and raced away.

10
THE HEALER

AS VÄINÖ DROVE ON toward a small village, blood flowed into the sleigh. He pulled up to the door of the first house and shouted, "Is there anyone here who can heal a cut from iron?"

A small boy got up from the stove bench and peered through the door. "There is no one here who can do that, but there is someone at another house."

Väinö drove to the next house and shouted at the window, "Is there anyone here who can stop the blood from an ax blow?"

An old woman with three teeth clicked them together and answered, "There is no one here who can do that, but there is someone at another house."

Väinö snapped the whip and the reindeer brought him to the farmyard of a greybearded man, who helped

Väinö into his home. "What mighty man are you? There is a sleigh full of blood out there."

"I am a pitiful man who needs a healer to close this ax wound," said Väinämöinen.

"Bigger things have been shut," said the man. "I know some healing words, and I have gathered grasses from journeys to nine soothsayers. But I cannot help you because, as everyone knows, I must begin with the origin of the thing that hurt you. I do not know the story of iron."

"I know it," said Väinö, "and I shall tell you now.

"When Ukko, the Creator, rubbed his hands together and pressed them down on his knee, the air maidens were born. One nursed the earth with her milk, and and it fed the iron egg of the beginning of things until it grew.

"Fire was Iron's wild and horrible cousin. In fear of him, Iron hid himself in a bog for many ages—sprawling under the heath, under the tree roots, under the nests of water birds.

"This was the place where the blacksmith Ilmarinen was born one night out of a hill of coal—with a copper hammer in one hand and a pair of tongs in the other. He built his smithy and made his forge and his bellows. He found a piece of bog iron and started to drop it into his fire.

"Iron was frightened. 'Don't worry,' the smith explained, 'fire will not destroy his own kin. When you pass through fire you will become beautiful and useful—

as ornaments and tools.' So Iron was melted as thin as gruel, and he cried to be taken out of the forge.

"'If I take you out,' said Ilmarinen, 'you will be so sharp and strong that you could do terrible things—even strike your own brother.'

"Iron swore an oath by the forge and by the anvil that he would always be peaceful. 'There is enough wood and stone for me to chop and chip, so that I do not need to eat my kin.'

"The craftsman snatched the soft iron from the fire, laid it on the anvil and worked it into sharp-edged tools. So that they would harden, he prepared a tempering mixture of lye and ashes in water. He called to a bee buzzing around his workshop, 'My honest, hardworking friend, bring a drop of honey to seal this sweet promise.'

"A wasp, servant of Hiisi the evil-doer, saw that the things being made were useful for mischief. So, before the bee returned, he buzzed back, carrying poison. He dropped it into the iron-tempering liquid. When the smith put the hot tools into the terrible mixture, it was hardened into the metal. And so Iron became angry when he came out of the forge. He forgot his promise and cut his clan, bit his kin and made blood flow everywhere."

The old man shook his head and said, "So that's what happened. Iron! That's how you came to think of yourself as so big and bad. You were not so fierce when you were milky rust in the swamp under the goose nests. For ages you were walked over by elk, beaten by the hooves of wild reindeer, trampled by the claws of wolves and bears. There wasn't much to you when you were dug up out of the bog and melted in the fire. When you were formed you swore an oath by the forge. A broken promise holds no power over this cut."

The healer turned to Väinämöinen and began to chant.

Blood, hold your gushing; stop your flow,
Steady—like a rock, a boulder,
You're splashing on an old man's beard!
Your course is to run among the bones,
Better for you within the skin,
Than seeping like a leaking boat.

You're no river, you have duties,
If you don't stop, I'll boil you still.
I know spells to stop the torrent.
If they don't work, I'll call Ukko.
Creator, come where you are needed,
Close the hole with your fat thumb.

With that, the bleeding stopped. Then the healer stirred together the ingredients for his cure. He boiled them down in a pot over the fire. To see if it was ready, he splashed some on a split aspen branch. The broken tree grew whole. He rubbed a little on a broken rock, and the halves joined together. Then he anointed the deep wound on Väinämöinen's knee. At once the flesh joined together and his leg was new. Väinö leapt for the door.

"Not so quick, my mighty man," said the healer. "Do not leave before you give thanks to the Ukko. And one more thing. No good can come from going about your business with bragging."

11
THE SAMPO

WHEN VÄINÄMÖINEN'S HOMELAND came into view, the moon hung so low over the spruce trees that it seemed to hang from their branches—along with Karhu, the bear stars. He could not stop to breathe in their beauty because he had promised the smith Ilmarinin to Louhi. He drove on to the smithy and called out over the clinking, clanging and hammering, "Ho, my brother Ilmari!"

"Hey, Väinämöinen, where have you been so long? Tell me all about your travels," said Ilmari at his forge.

"I have been to Pohjola, to North Farm, where I met a maiden who shines from all sides. Never have I seen so beautiful a creature, and she has not found a man good enough to be her husband. You, Ilmari, are the man. All you have to do is forge a mill, a sampo, from a barleycorn and you will get her as your payment. It's that simple."

"I know you, Väinö. You have made some kind of a bargain. Well, you can forget about it. Never, for a long forever, will I go to that cold, dark place."

"There's more," said Väinö, thinking fast. "You can have the moon as well as the bear stars out of a spruce tree by my field. Come, you only have to climb up and get them!"

The skeptical blacksmith followed his old friend, and, sure enough, the moon and stars looked as though they sat in the trees. Ilmari climbed, but before he could reach the moon, Väinö sang up a breeze under his breath and conjured the wind into a gale which blew the poor smith all the way to Pohjola. Ilmarinin flew on a whirling, swirling journey high up over the moon and across the shoulders of the bear stars. He landed in the snow on the path to Louhi's sauna.

"What manner of man arrives on the wind?" inquired Louhi. "You did not even wake the dog. Have you ever heard of Ilmarinen the great blacksmith, whom we are waiting for?"

"I am Ilmarinen, and I shall leave just as I have come."

"What you need is to get warmed up in the sauna," said Louhi. "Then come have a bite to eat before you go." The old woman hurried ahead up the path to the house to get ready.

"Daughter, Ilmarinen is here to make the magic mill, the sampo which will grind out all that we need. Put

on your soft white dress, your bright shoulder brooches, your copper tasseled sash, and frame your fair face with ornaments in your hair." Then Louhi stoked up the fire and set to baking piiraka, the little salmon pastries offered in Kaleva when a mother approves of a suitor.

The maid of North Farm opened the door to the Kalavalander, her eyes aglow, her cheeks blushing. Soon he was full of food and drink and love. Louhi said, "Smith, if you can make a sampo from a barleycorn, a mill which will grind riches, then you can have this maiden in return."

"Perhaps I can," he agreed. But he found no forge there, no anvil, no bellows, no hammer. "How do these women run this place without any tools?" he snorted, as he set up on a slab of stone. He used the wind to blow his fire as he stoked and fueled it for days.

Bad things came out of the red glow—a bow that would shoot a person every day, a boat that would go to war without reason, a plow that would turn good grain down into the earth. The craftsman smashed these things and shoved the broken bits back into the fire. The fire spit, sparks flashed, ashes floated to the sky. At last the smith leaned over the forge and dropped in Louhi's barleycorn. Then he watched the sampo forming in the bottom of the forge. When he lifted it out, it was colored with a thousand hues of the fire. Ilmarinen shaped it and decorated the lid. When he worked the mill, out came a binful of grain to eat, a binful of grain to store, and a binful to sell. Out came salt and coins and food for a feast.

Louhi hopped on her skis and chuckled as she carried the sampo all the way to her secret vault on Copper Mountain. She shoveled aside the scree and opened each of the nine locked copper doors deep within the granite cave.

Ilmarinen was happy, too. He went to Louhi's daughter and asked, "Now that the sampo is complete, will you marry me and come to Kaleva?"

"No," said the maiden, "I cannot leave my mother with all the summer tasks. The berries will hang unpicked, and there will be no one to wake the birds and start them singing."

Ilmarinen was brooding when Louhi returned from stowing her treasure. "Why is your hat all crooked, smith?" she asked. He told her that her daughter would not have him.

"Now that's too bad," said Louhi. "Would you like to go home?"

"I want to go to die of a broken heart," said Ilmarinen.

Louhi put him in the stern of a boat, gave him a basket of leftover piirakas and a paddle, and shoved him off downstream toward the ocean. After him she sent a wind which carried him south to his home.

Days later, when Väinämöinen saw the seasick smith landing in the boat alone, the storysinger knew he had another chance at the lovely daughter of Louhi.

12
DEATH'S ISLAND

VÄINÄMÖINEN WASTED NO TIME in finishing the boat the maiden had ordered him to make from her distaff. But the ship must launch itself, she had told him. Väinö knew no magic to do such a thing. "Who would know the right charm?" he wondered.

First he went to the swans and the geese. They did not know a charm to make a boat launch itself, but they taught him their transformation spell—the one they use to change from eggs to birds. He went to the reindeer and the squirrels. They did not know magic for moving a boat, but they taught him a spell to know which direction to escape danger.

"Who knows the most mysterious magic spells? Death knows them!" thought the storysinger, and started off for Tuonela, Death's island, to learn them. It was a week's journey by foot through thorny brush to the ink-black river which flowed by its shores. When Väinö got there, he cried out, "Boatman, come over and get me."

Death's skinny daughter was washing black clothes in the black water. "What brings you here, since you are not dead?"

"Iron brought me here," said Väinö.

"Now that's a lie," she replied. "If a blow from iron had brought you here, your clothes would be bloody."

"Water brought me here," said Väinö.

"What a liar," said Death's daughter. "If water had done you in, it would be dripping from your hems."

"Fire brought me here," said Väinö.

"Another lie," she answered. "If fire had brought you here, your collar would be scorched and your bushy beard would be singed. Tell me the truth now, if you want me to bring you over here. Out with it."

"Well," said Väinö, "I lied a tiny bit, but I can also tell the truth. I am making a boat, and I came to Tuonela to borrow an auger."

"Without dying you want to enter Death's domain? I thought you were a fool, but you are worse than a fool—you're a madman. Better for you to go home."

"A woman would change her mind. It takes a man to follow through."

"Hmpf," said Death's daughter, who rowed over and brought him back to the island. As he leaned forward

to put his foot on the dark shore, she whispered in his ear, "You can't go back again."

Death's wife, in tattered black and gray, greeted him with a two-handled urn. "Drink up! What makes you come so soon?"

Väinö looked down into the cup. The bottom of the brown brew was crawling with worms and maggots. "No, thank you," he said, "I haven't come here to rot. I'm here for a charm."

"Death does not give away his magic, nor do I," said his wife. "But I shall give you a sample." She waved her hand over his head, and he fell into a drowsy swoon. All day he lay motionless, watching Death's son stringing iron nets with his three hooked, metal-tipped fingers. He stretched the nets across the black river—crosswise, lengthwise, and aslant—to prevent the living visitor from escaping Death's abode. Väinö saw that there was no escape.

At once he remembered the transformation charm that he learned from the geese. He whispered it under his breath and turned himself into an eel, slithering to the shore. He was just small enough to slip through the maze of nets. He used the deer's escape charm to find his way in the blackness to the other shore.

The next morning, when Death's son went out to check his nets, he found a catch of a hundred sea trout. But he did not get the big fish Väinämöinen .

13
IN THE BELLY OF THE GIANT

OLD VÄINÖ ESCAPED Death's Island with his life, but not with the spell he went for. No one knew magic like Death, thought Väinö, no one but the giant Antero Vipunen. Vipunen was a hoarder, and just as he consumed animals and men, he devoured spells and charms. In the treasure chest of his memory were a thousand magic verses. Surely among them must be the spell Väinö needed to launch his boat for the maiden.

The way to the giant was not a pleasant journey. The route wound first over a path of needlepoints, then along a road of sword blades, and finally around a cliff-edge of battle-axes. So Väinö went to the blacksmith and asked, "Dear Ilmarinen, will you forge me some iron shoes? I am setting out to walk the road of sharp blades to visit Antero Vipunen."

"It has been many years since that giant has lain in wait to pluck travelers off the road and eat them," said Ilmarinen. "He disappeared a long time ago. You'll get no magic from him—not half a word. But if you insist on going, I'd better make you more than iron shoes. I'll make you a byrnie—a coat of mail—and a stout sword, too."

So Väinö set out in heavy iron boots forged by the smithy. He trudged over the needle points. He tramped over the sword blades. He stomped over the ax blades, all the while keeping a sharp eye out for Vipunen. But the giant was nowhere to be seen. Väinö walked up a big wooded hill to get a better look around. As he climbed, the hill began to shake. He held on to a tree with his arms and legs as the hilltop sank and rose up again. A rumbling noise came from a gaping hole further along the moving ridge. Above the hole, Väinö saw an enormous nose and two closed eyes. So! The giant had been sleeping so long that aspens grew across his shoulders and birches rose from his eyebrows. The willows were so thick on his chin that there was no way to tell where his beard left off. Spruce and pine meandered all over his belly. The old giant lolled in the landscape, a cone-filled fir tree growing between his teeth.

Up the breathing belly Väinämöinen stumbled, grabbing at branches and landing in a thicket on Vipunen's chin. Väinö scrambled to the edge of the yawning cavern that was the giant's mouth. Between teeth covered with moss and ferns, air rushed in , forcing the giant's fleshy throat to roar until his jaw rattled. His breath swooshed out with such force that a squirrel was blown out of a berry bush in his nose all the way to a grove of pine in his armpit. Väinämöinen smacked the mammoth teeth of the sleeping giant with his sword and hollered, "Wake up, you lazy lout!"

Vipunen woke up. He bit off the tiny sword. Then he took two quick breaths and sneezed. Väinö was hurled into the air on a wave of spray. He tumbled down, one heavy boot sliding over the giant's round wet lip, pulling him over the edge onto the purple tongue below. The giant gulped him down, sword hilt and all. A deafening word passed Väinö as he fell down the slimy tunnel to the giant's stomach: "Delicious!"

Väinö tromped around in a pool of putrid smelling acid and poked his broken sword at the leathery tripe walls in the belly of Vipunen. The giant took no notice of his presence, aside from remarking that, of the hundreds of men that he had eaten, this one was the tastiest.

"This does not look good," thought Väinö. So he set to work. First he conjured a boat from an undigested cowhide. Then he paddled the length of the foul lake from the throat to the gut-end, gathering bones of those who had come before him. He laid out his chain-mail byrnie on the shore and piled the bones on top of it. From his shirtsleeve he made a bellows, from his sock he made the mouthpiece, from his pants leg he shredded fuel, and from bones he made fire sticks. There, in the belly of the great magician, Väinö rubbed the fire sticks, blowing on them gently until a spark began to blaze.

The giant had settled back to sleep when the first

wisp of smoke tickled his nose and the cinders began to choke his throat. The chain mail under the fire began to melt and drip hot iron onto the lining of his stomach. The giant sat up, ripping leagues of roots out of the earth, toppling trees, and scattering animals from the tilting terrain. Väinämöinen kept pumping air on his fire.

The giant howled, "Who is hooked in to me? What kind of fool would wake a sleeping giant? Are you a ghost? A disease? An illusion? Are you a hired fiend? Are you the demon Hiisi's brat just out for practice?

"If that's who you are, I have the power to send you back to Hiisi's lair. Let me know when you get home by kicking over the outhouse, grabbing up your evil master and twisting his head around. If that's not where you come from, I'll propel you east to swim the whirlpool at Finnmark where whole trees are sucked in, roots up. Or I can conjure you down to Tuonela, to the black river. From there you never can escape."

The giant choked on the smoke. "If you need a horse to leave, I'm glad to conjure one of Demon Hiisi's. You won't mind if he gets a little angry. Or, if you prefer, I'll get you his alder wood skis; they come with one ski pole which will scatter anything in your path.

"Do you get the feeling you're not wanted, you motherless pest? Night is ending, and demons must be gone before dawn. If this is my time to die, so be it, but I refuse to die from indigestion."

"Why, Vaipunen," hollered Väinö, "I am just getting settled in my new home. My plan is to stay forever. A stew of liver, lungs and belly fat is what I have in mind, followed by a fillet of heart. But I could be persuaded to

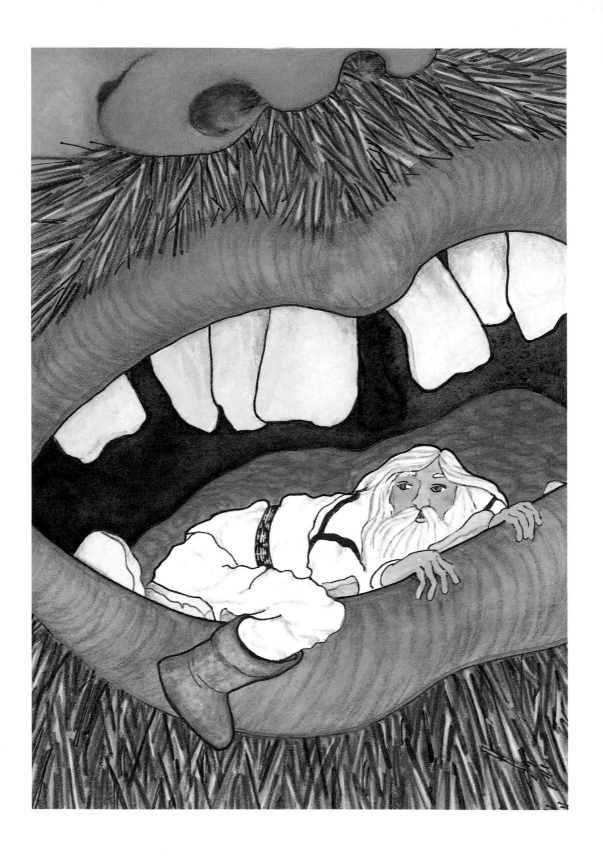

feast on your knowledge instead. You can be free of me if you will chant your magic verses."

The giant wheezed a cloud of smoke and agreed. It was a cheap price for one who wanted no more than to get back to sleep. He opened his trove of stories, charms and incantations. For the entire day and night he sang, beginning at the beginning of time, chanting songs no longer sung to children or understood by men. He sang of the creator, Ukko, and how, by his will, air was created out of itself, and how out of air came water. He sang about the rising of the moon from a broken egg, and the rising of the sun from its yolk. He told how the earth was formed by Ilmatar, the daughter of Air. Then he sang of the birth of her son Väinämöinen, born an old man:

> *Such a man who had no childhood,*
> *Never learned to play and love,*
> *Is forever somber, searching,*
> *But for what he cannot know.*

The words leapt from the giant's mouth, phrases tripped nimbly over his fat tongue, stories rolled out of his dreams. He sang spells to halt the sun, still the moon, hold the sea waves and the ripples in bay, to stem the rivers and give pause to the great rapids. He sang of spells for tasks great and small—for sowing seeds, for making pulla bread rise and laying logs for a house. And a charm to launch a boat.

As soon as Väinö heard that, he hollered, "Vipunen, open up your mouth wide and I will leave you."

Out climbed Väinö over the violet gums and brambly maw as quickly as he could haul the iron boots behind him. He found himself standing before an eye a fathom high. It blinked. The giant said, "I have devoured and destroyed a thousand things, but nothing like you. I should have guessed it was you, Väinämöinen, come to gather songs and charms for your collection. Well, you got what you wanted in a disagreeable way. Get going before I tell your mother."

But Väinö had already leapt over the hedge along the giant's ear, down the grove on his shoulder, and through the willows that grew all the way to his belt. There he let himself down to the ground on a branch and ran for his life. He was already across the hatchets, over the sword blades and past the needles when the giant mumbled, "You have not heard the half of it, Väinämöinen!"

14
THE RACE

IT WAS DARK WHEN Väinö reached home. But he was on the riverbank at sunrise to launch his boat for the journey to Pohjola to claim his bride. He pulled the pinewood chocks out from the rollers under his boat. Then he climbed on board and spoke the giant's spell. With the words, the craft slipped over the bark-stripped logs into the river. As the current carried the ship toward the sea, Väinö hoisted the sail and settled in for the journey.

Annikki, the blacksmith's sister, was up before dawn washing clothes at the headland. She saw a new boat sailing out of the mouth of the river. As it rounded the spit, she called,

"Hey, Väinö, where are you setting out to?"

"I'm setting out to go salmon fishing, sister of the smith!"

"Don't try to lie to me, Väinö. I know about salmon fishing. Your boat has no nets or lines along its side, no spears under the thwart, no long poles in its stern. Where are you heading out to, old man?"

Väinö answered, "I'm going to hunt geese."

"Did you think I would believe that, Väinö? I know about hunting geese. You have no big crossbow strung and drawn and no black dog on a leash at the prow. Where are you really going?"

"I'm going to war."

"I know about war, too. You'd have a hundred men, with weapons ready under the rowing benches. You had better tell me what you are up to or I'll tip your bow under."

"Well, Annikki, I see that I can't get going with a little fib. The truth is that I'm on my way to Pohjola to marry a maiden at North Farm. Wish me luck!"

Annikki did not wish him luck. She dropped her unrinsed kerchiefs on the shore. With wet hands she pulled up her skirts and ran to her brother's workshop.

Ilmarinen, covered with soot, was decorating a brooch with silver figures.

"Brother," said Annikki, "if you leave off making love gifts long enough to fix my broken belt clasp, I shall tell you something you need to know."

"For good news, I'll fix your clasp," laughed the smith. "For bad news, I'll toss it into the forge."

"Since you returned from North Farm," said Anniki, "you have tapped away the days forging things for courting—shoes for the horse, runners for the sled, gifts for the girl. It may be too late," she continued, as she held on tight to her belt. "Väinämöinen is on his way by sea to claim your bride."

Ilmari's heart felt heavier than his hammer. "My little sister, heat the sauna while I repair your clasp. Make enough soap to wash the cinders from a winter's work out of my skin."

Annikki gathered the things she needed for the sauna: wood, rocks, water, birch twigs, ashes. With the wood, she built a fire to heat the rocks and make the water rise up in steam. With the birch twigs, she tied a bath whisk and softened it against a rock. With the ash, she made lathery soap, sweet enough to bathe a bridegroom.

In the sauna, Ilmari scrubbed his grimy body and poured water over himself by the bucketful until his hair was flaxen and his cheeks were red. Anniki hardly recognized the clean, pale man who came out of the steam when the door opened.

She had laid out his linen shirt and his blue homespun topcoat, together with his sturdy leather boots, soft stockings, and the belt woven by his mother when she was a girl. He looked every bit the proper suitor when he put a high-peaked hat on his golden hair. In his sled he laid a bearskin robe. He harnessed his fastest colt and hung the traces with bird-shaped bells to sing him on his way.

He drove swiftly through hills and gullies, and along the sandy dunes by the sea. For days gravel stung his eyes and the sea spray came up in his face. Still he drove on until he saw the sail of Väinämöinen's boat. He startled the old man with his cry, "Hey, old Väinö! I have paid my bride price, and you are going after my bride!" His horse began to gallop ahead of the boat.

"Ho, Ilmari, I have paid the price as well. So let's be friends."

"If a friend is someone who blows me to a frozen wasteland and then sneaks off to capture my love, then I can do without him," yelled Ilmarinen.

"Since one of us must lose the girl, we can agree not to lose a friend as well. Suppose we let her choose, and promise not to bear a grudge."

"Fair enough. Agreed!" shouted Ilmari, as he raced on ahead.

They traveled on, each on his own journey and each driven on by the other—first the blacksmith in the lead and then the storysinger. The sails filled, the sea hummed, the stallion ran, the bird bells sang.

Already the spotted dog at North Farm had begun to bark, her tail sweeping the ground. "Who is coming both by land and by sea?" wondered Louhi. "Toss a rowan stick into the fire. If blood streams out of it, war is coming; if water flows out of it, we will have peace." But instead honey flowed out of the stick. "That means suitors!" cried Louhi in delight, and she raced down to the

riverbank, where the dog was gazing seaward. She strained her eyes and saw a great ship racing with full sail unfurled against a galloping stallion pulling a sleigh. "Come, daughter," called Louhi. "The silver-haired Väinämöinen and the golden-haired Ilmarinen are on their way to claim a bride. Which do you choose?"

"Mother, I choose not to marry."

"The time has come, my sweet one. Since you will not choose, the choice is mine. When they arrive, I will bring honey wine in a two-eared cup and put it in the hands of one. Väinämöinen the magician will drink from the cup and be my kin."

"Oh, Mamma," cried the maiden, "I will not be sold for spells or songs. I can't marry an old man. If I must marry, I will marry the younger one."

"Oh, child, if you marry the smith you will live in a sooty house with sooty children and spend your days scrubbing with a bucket of dark water."

"I would rather roll in coal than be wife to an aged man. It is better to be buried in dirt than in boredom."

Ilmari reached North Farm first, but the sleigh found no place to ford the river. Väinämöinen won the race because he could row upstream to the farmhouse. He beached his boat, stalked up to the cabin, flung open the door, and said, "Now will you marry me?"

"Well," said the girl, "have you made a boat out of my spindle which can launch itself?"

"At the risk of losing my life, I have built from your spindle a boat which holds steady against a headwind, cuts through the ocean waves, sails smoothly on the open sea and rides as lightly as a bubble. I have launched it on its own with a spell come by at great trouble. Yes, I have done all that!" cried Väinö.

"Well," said Louhi's daughter, "I could never marry a seafaring man." She slipped out and left her mother to deal with the suitors.

15
PLOWING SNAKES

ILMARINEN STRAIGHTENED his fine blue jacket
and knocked at the farmhouse door. Louhi peered
out, and he asked for the maiden of North Farm.

"Not so fast, blacksmith," said Louhi. "Perhaps you
can claim your bride when you have done a few chores."

"Certainly," said Ilmarinen. "How may I help?"

"First, plow the field of serpents," replied Louhi.

Ilmarinen, weary from the race and discouraged by
the old woman, went to find her daughter. "Remember
me?" he said, "When I forged the mill which grinds out
the grain for your table, I was promised you as my bride.
But your mother has set me to plowing a field full of poison snakes before I can claim you."

"It is not my choice to marry anyone," said the
maiden. "But if I can get out of marrying the old man by

helping you, I will do it. First you must forge a plow. Put your ear close, and I will whisper a spell that I have learned from my mother."

Ilmarinen stoked up the fire in his stone forge at North Farm and hammered out a plow. He hitched it to his lively horse. The plow lifted the snakes, their heads rearing and hissing, to the tops of the furrows. He chanted the snake charm, and the serpents writhed harmlessly as the plow passed.

When he finished, he went to Louhi and said, "Now I have turned over the snake-filled earth. May I now take my wife?"

"Not so soon, smith," said Louhi. "Before you do that you must capture the demon Hiisi's terrible bear."

Ilmari went to the maiden and told her this news. "That is more difficult," she said. "First you must forge a bit and shackles. Lean over and I will whisper a spell that I have learned from my mother."

The smith went back to his forge and made the things to hold the bear. Then he went to the lair of Hiisi and his bear. There he lay in wait. Hiisi came out, a tiny demon with a round head, a pointed nose and a bony body. Ilmari dared not breathe. When he heard an immense growl, he chanted the spell. A fog descended, making him invisible. When the bear came out, Ilmari leapt up and shackled the animal, leaving the demon hollering in the mist.

He knocked on Louhi's door. "Here I am, dame, and here is your bear. I am ready to claim your daughter."

"Not in such a hurry," said Louhi. "One more thing.

Catch the ancient pike swimming around Death's island—without a line and without a net."

"And then I shall have my bride?"

"Only then," said Louhi.

Ilmari went to the maiden for her help.

"My mother knows a spell to turn herself into a bird," she told him, "but I do not know it. I can only teach you to call for the help of the eagle. Since you cannot use a line or a net, the bird could catch the pike."

Soon the bird with great wings was descending in a spiral over North Farm. The eagle agreed to help Ilmari. The smith fitted him with claws as long as pitchforks and climbed onto the bird's back. They flew all the way to Tuonela. Nothing could be seen under the surface of the horrible black water that surrounded Death's island, so Ilmari leaned down and dragged his hand under the water. Around the island he trolled until his fingers caught on the rough scales of the pike.

At the same time, the pike found him. The fish leapt from the water, seized him with huge jaws and pulled him off the back of the eagle with a quick yank. The pike dragged him quickly under water, down to the ooze at the bottom of the river. Ilmari struggled, and the fish swam back up to get a better grip on the man. The bird grabbed the fish, but he lost hold, and Ilmari was plunged down into the murky water again.

The eagle hovered, looking with sharp eyes into the darkness. Suddenly, the bird sank its talons, their curves as sharp as scythes, into the backbone of the fish. He pulled the water creature into the air. The fish, thrashing with Ilmari in his mouth, was carried into an oak tree. As Ilmari was grasping for branches to pull himself out of the fish's jaws, the eagle began to eat the fish.

"Stop!" cried the blacksmith. "I have to bring this thing back to Louhi."

"We'll bring her the head," said the eagle, with his mouth full.

And so Ilmarinen brought the gift of a fish head to his future mother-in-law. "Maybe you can make a chair out of it," he said hopefully. "I've tilled the adders, bridled the bear, and caught the fish. Now may I claim my bride?"

Louhi sighed. "I would have done well to have hidden my daughter away in a weaving shed to keep away you wooing Finns. I cannot choose her husband. She ends up with a sooty blacksmith. I end up with a fish-head. So be it. Let the preparations for the marriage celebration begin! Go now, bridegroom, and invite everyone to the feast."

The wedding at North Farm was the biggest party anyone had ever known. Louhi ground out a banquet from the sampo: barley for bread and beer, yellow mustard, wheat for salmon crust, soft butter, sweet honey and cream cakes. Guests arrived from near and far. Louhi saw that no person was left out. Some guests walked with straw stuffed in their woven birch shoes; some came in decorated sleighs. The spotted dog barked as they approached, and it was days before she curled up in front of the hall door in exhaustion.

Fifty guests arrived pulling an ox by a long rope tied to its horn. The ox was so big, they said, that it took all

day for a fly to go around its legs. They roasted it on a spit made from a whole evergreen log and made fathoms of sausages for the party. When Ilmari was seated at the head of the table and all the guests had bowls brim full and dishes spilling over with food, Louhi asked, "Who will sing? What is a wedding without song?"

A shy boy sang a little verse. An old storysinger from the village, his voice as dry as an old stream bed, started, but he lost interest when the sausages were served.

"Let us have Väinämöinen, the greatest storysinger of them all," said Louhi.

"If no one else here will do it, than I shall begin," said Väinö. He started with a sad song about how an old man can never beat a young man in a contest for love. Everyone cried. But he sang more—until the women were laughing and the men were smiling. Late into the night the guests listened in wonder as one song after another flowed from the storysinger. At dawn he ended with, "Let there be no regrets."

But there were regrets. The maiden regretted that she had bargained away her freedom to avoid marrying an old man. "Mother, I have changed my mind," said the maiden. "I was like a flying bird, a fluttering leaf, a shooting spark. Now I'm leaving behind my wild daydreams. I have one foot in my bridegroom's sleigh, but the foot on my own threshold has grown heavy."

"Lean over and I will whisper a spell I learned from my mother," said the matriarch of North Farm, as she bade her daughter goodbye.

Ilmarinen sped along, one hand guiding the stallion, the other holding his young bride in his arm. His sleigh skimmed the shores of Pohjola and the sandy ridges of Lapland. On the third day, he saw the smoke from the cabins of Kaleva. When he pointed out his home, the young woman stood up in the moving sleigh, let the lap robe fall, stepped up onto the seat and rose into the sky in the form of a bird.

Old and young Kalevalanders were waiting to catch sight of the smith and his beautiful wife from Pohjola. "I have heard that she grew from a strawberry," said one. "Her eyes are like the stars, her brows curved like the moon."

A child was the first to hear the bells on the sapling sleigh shafts. An old man shouted, "Welcome! We did not know if you had to stay in the frozen north to wait for a little bride to grow up or fatten up a skinny one!" But when the sleigh drew closer and the crowd could see inside, they saw only Ilmarinen. Beside him was a pile of soft cloth and jewelry forged by a heartsick lover—gold bangles, necklaces and belts, rings, golden braid, a brooch—all gleaming from an empty shawl. Above him, rising high in the air and turning toward the North, flew a bird.

"There she goes," said the smith.

16
THE SEA BATTLE FOR THE SAMPO

THERE WERE more regrets. Väinämöinen regretted losing the contest for a bride, and Ilmarinin regretted marrying a maiden who had turned into a bird.

"Well, friend," said Väinö, "let us go and claim the sampo."

"There is no way to get the sampo. It is hidden under the scree in a granite cave behind Louhi's nine locks in Copper Mountain," answered the blacksmith.

"Come on, we'll figure out how to do it as we sail."

"The sea is too dangerous, Väinö," said Ilmari, whose last trip home in Louhi's boat was enough for him. "A storm would leave us rowing with our fingers, steering with our palms for rudders. Travel on land is safer."

"Safe but tedious. I was born at sea, Ilmari, but if I must travel with a landlubber, so be it."

As the smith was loading the sleigh, he heard a cry-ing noise. He followed the sound and discovered Väinämöinen's boat wailing, "I yearn for the water as if my heart will break."

"Väinö, Väinö," called Ilmari, as he ran up the path. "We have to sail the boat!"

Väinö, who had been hidden inside the hull making the voices, appeared on the path behind him. "Anything for an old friend," said the storysinger.

The adventurers sailed north with ease—until their boat stopped dead in the water. Ilmari leaned so far over the side to see what was wrong that Väinö had to pull him back by his foot. Still, they saw neither a sand bar nor a dead tree. Väinö picked up his friend's sword, explaining that his had been bitten off by a giant, and swung it down under the boat. The sea turned crimson with blood. The severed front half of a pike came up on the end of the weapon. The boat surged forward, and the travelers feasted on fish.

When only bones were left, Väinö picked up the jaw of the pike. From it, he made a kantele, a harp, with the fish teeth for pegs and his own beard hairs for strings. He laid the harp over his knees and began to play. The music moved him to sing. He began to cry as he told of the maidens who got away. The tears, plump as peas, dropped from his eyes, rolled over his round cheeks, and into the sea. When the teardrops touched the ocean floor, they became blue pearls.

Once they reached Pohjola, Ilmarinin rowed and

Väinämöinen steered the boat up the river to North Farm. The spotted dog was barking, and Louhi was waiting on the shore.

"Back so soon?" asked Louhi.

"We have come to claim our sampo," said Ilmarinin.

"Not on your life," said Louhi. "It stays in Copper Mountain."

"Very well," said Väinö, and he offered to sing her a song on his fish-jaw harp.

"Splendid," said Louhi, who brought him inside the hall and settled down to listen with some guests who had stayed on after the wedding. She was enchanted by the music. Väinö sang of dusk, of night, of dreams and deep sleep. One by one, the guests closed their eyes. The old dame began to nod. At last she cradled her head in her arm and fell asleep across the table. Väinö and Illmari tip-toed out to find the sampo.

The Kalavalanders stood before the great doors in Copper Mountain, Väinö with his harp and Ilmari with a tub of lard from the storeroom. "I'll sing the doors open," said Väinö, as he sat down to play.

"That may work," said the blacksmith, "but I think it will help to grease the bolts in the locks and work them loose with a knife."

It took some singing and greasing and jiggling for the locks to open. They had made their way to the eighth door when the spotted dog woke up, stretched, and began to make her dawn rounds. When she discovered the for-eigners at the vault, she ran to wake her mistress.

"Sing fast," said Ilmari.

"You can't rush magic," said Väinö. "Try more lard."

They could hear the dog yapping up the sauna path. The eighth door swung open. The dog began to bark under Louhi's window. Sweat covered Väinö's forehead as he plucked the harp. The dog howled. The smith wearily slipped the last lock as Louhi's voice was heard calling from the yard, "Stop, thieves!" The guests shouted in confusion from the hall.

The last big door swung open and Väinö grabbed the sampo. He ran over locks and slipped on lard, racing down the sauna path to the river, jumping into his boat and dipping the oars just as Ilmari heaved himself in over the bow.

Louhi was furious. She called Fog Maiden and showed her the broken locks of her nine vaults. She explained that her land was barren without the sampo, and the thieves were escaping by boat. Fog Maiden loosened a dense mist from her sleeve and blew it to the sea.

One moment Väinö and Ilmari were sailing south swiftly in the sunlight. The next moment, the wind stopped, and a thick fog descended—so heavy that they could not see the tip of the mast. They sat becalmed and befuddled.

Louhi pushed her boat off its logs, raised the mast, and hoisted the sails. As she worked, she told North Wind the story of how her treasure house was broken into and her sampo stolen. North Wind sent her boat quickly after the Kalevalanders.

Väinö was still adrift, trying spells and charms to lift the mist. Finally, he picked up Ilmari's sword and, with both hands, sliced the fog cleanly in half in an arc over his head. It fell into the sea and revealed a clear sky. Ilmari shinnied up the mast and looked in every direction. "There is just one cloud left," he shouted.

"That is not a cloud, it is a sail!" cried Väinö, as he began to row furiously.

Louhi gained until the men could see wisps of white hair blowing across her bright eyes. "Give it up!" she shouted.

Väinämöinen knew he had met a magician who was his match. But there was one trick he remembered from the giant. He opened his tinder box and threw a pinch of dried moss over his left shoulder into the water.

May a reef rise under water,
Sheltering fish, trapping ships.

Louhi's boat came hurtling on. Suddenly it ran into the unseen island and shattered. The mast snapped and the sails fell flapping. Louhi leaped into the water and tried to put her boat back together. She swam from rib to plank, but they were in splinters. Väinö and Ilmari were rowing hard to get away when they heard a loud cry.

Louhi had changed herself into a bird with a head like a hawk. In that form, she rode the wreckage of her boat until she had armored her wings and her claws with pieces she found there. Then, the heavily laden creature labored to lift herself into the air, screeching. The bird hovered over the ship, the shadow of her outstretched wings reaching across the deck.

Ilmari was terrified. "I didn't think we should come by sea."

Väinö shouted to the bird, "How about sharing the sampo?"

The unwieldly wings grew heavy, and Louhi came to rest at the top of the mast. The weight of her armor of timber was so great that the ship began to list to one side.

"Never!" she answered.

The boat began to keel over and Väinö's fish jaw harp slid across the deck. The blacksmith and the story-singer grabbed for it, but the harp slipped overboard, lost to the sea. Louhi swooped down and plucked up the sampo with her claws. As the boat began to capsize, Ilmari leaped up and grabbed for the sampo. His great hand knocked it from Louhi's claw, and it fell, hitting the side of the boat and shattering into pieces.

The useless lid rolled across the deck, and the great bird snatched it up, weeping. "That was the harvest of North Farm, dropped into the sea." She held the lid close to her scaly breast, her great wings flapping, as she turned northward.

Pieces of the sampo were strewn along the shore of Kaleva. Big chunks of the mill had fallen into the water, giving the Finns unending riches from the ocean. Väinö gathered the small shards and crumbled fragments washed up by the waves. He sowed them across the land, making it fertile. Seeds sprang up, and the sun shone on Finland's sweet soil.

"Now it is time to sing for joy," said Väinö. "If I only had a harp."

17
HOW LOUHI BROUGHT
WINTER TO FINLAND

AMIDST THE GOOD NEW LIFE in Kaleva—trees blooming, grain growing—Väinämöinen sat under the birch in his field and wept for his lost harp. He had spent days in his boat raking the sea. He pulled up driftwood and seaweed, but no harp. "My joy is gone," he cried.

"My joy is gone, too," sang the clear, sweet voice of the curly birch tree. "My twigs are cut for sauna whisks, my bark is woven into baskets and my branches are burned for fire." And so it was that the birch found its voice as a new harp made by Väinämöinen. The story-singer carved pegs from an oak where the cukoo sang. Down among the shore rocks where the mermaids groom themselves, Väinö found five hairs to make the strings.

Väinö leaned the new harp on his shoulder and tuned it. When the sound was true and pure, he laid the kantele gently across his knees, lowered his fingers to the strings and began to play a tune. The curly birch wood sang, the cukoos chirped in the oak pegs and the hairs of the mermaids rejoiced.

First the squirrels hurried out to hear, leaping from branch to branch. The weasles, the elk and the lynxes turned toward the sound. The bear rose from his den, the wolf trotted around the swamp to listen. Sampsa the woodland spirit nestled in the crotch of a tree. Little finches and flocks of larks settled in the branches. Sea

ducks gathered along the shore, salmon gathered from rocky hiding places and whitefish rose from the ocean depths. All creatures running on four legs or hopping on two crouched upon their paws to hear. Even worms crawled closer to the surface, and tree stumps rocked in place. Teary-eyed women put down their work and ran to join men leaning on grub hoes. Never before had they heard such sounds. Never had they felt such joy.

Louhi heard that the pieces of the sampo had spread good fortune in Kaleva. She heard that Väinämöinen didn't stop singing even to change his shirt. North Farm

was barren since the sampo was stolen. There was no more grain. The guests were gone. Louhi was angry. She began to scheme revenge on Kaleva.

Her days were spent trying spells for one terrible thing after another: iron hailstones and Death's grandchildren: Colic, Gout and Plague. But the good fortune of Kaleva was too strong for her magic, and Väinämöinen just kept on singing.

The sun and the moon had been listening to Väinö, and they decided to come closer so that they could hear better. The moon descended into a crooked birch tree. The sun came down to the crown of an old pine. When Louhi learned of that, she turned herself into a bird and flew to Kaleva, scooped up the sun and the moon and took them back to North Farm. There she hid them in Copper Mountain, behind nine new locks with immovable bolts.

Dark came to Kaleva. The days and nights were all the same. Crops wilted, the cattle huddled together in the cold and the singing stopped altogether. Children came to Ilmarinin and asked him to forge a new sun and a new moon; the blacksmith did it to stop their crying. He hung the metal discs in the trees where the sun and moon had come to listen. But the golden sun did not shine and the silver moon did not glow.

Väinämöinen laid out the divining sticks to find out where the sun and moon were hidden. The sticks said that they were imprisoned in the Northland in Copper Mountain behind nine locks with immovable bolts. Nothing could be done.

Louhi became so curious to see what misery had

befallen Kaleva that she turned herself back into a bird and flew south. She was drawn to the light of the smithy window and perched on the sill. The craftsman recognized Louhi, and he asked sweetly, "What are you doing here, pretty bird?"

"I have come to see what you are making, smith," replied Louhi.

"I am making an iron collar for the witch of North Farm. We will chain her safely to the side of Copper Mountain," said Ilmari, who was doing no such thing.

"The mistress of North Farm is not a witch, Kaleva-lander. She may be old and gap-toothed, she may be wily and tough from the harsh cold, wizened by the barren land, made clever by the struggle to survive, and she may have learned some useful magic. She may be angry, too, that her sampo has been stolen. But she is no witch."

"Only a witch would hide the sun and the moon," said Ilmari. "I am forging the chain which will hold Louhi forever on Copper Mountain."

This frightened Louhi. She knew that Väinämöinen and Ilmarinen were clever enough to catch her. She turned from the smith's sill and flew north without resting. When she got to North Farm, she became a crone again. She scratched away the snow, cleared the scree and opened the nine locks to her vault. She turned her head away from the blinding light as the sun and the moon rose out of the mountain. Then she called Wind, who found Louhi in her barren treasure house. Wind agreed to carry something more to Kaleva. Along with the sun and moon, Louhi sent Winter—the fierce, long, freezing Northland Winter.

18
VÄINÄMÖINEN'S PROMISE

SUMMER CAME, and the Finns were blessed by the shards of the sampo. Berries, nuts and grains bulged in baskets, and in midsummer the sun shone all night. But life was hard in winter. The light dimmed to darkness, and bone-biting cold descended on Kaleva. Food ran short, and so did good will.

Sometimes, when the land no longer gave the people everything they needed, difficult decisions had to be made among them. Although he protested that he was only a storysinger, old Väinämöinen was chosen as the best to judge matters that had no easy answer. So it happened that Väinö was sitting next to his fire, singing and plucking his kantele, as he did in the dark of winter, when there was a knock at his cabin door. An old man, bent and on skis, leaned on his single pole.

"I need the elder sage with ancient knowledge," he said. Väinö took the man in, warmed him and fed him from meager food stores, and listened to his story. Then he saw him off in the grey afternoon.

The next morning, the light was dim when Väinö opened the curtain of his bed and peered out of the small moss-chinked window. Long icicles hung from his sod roof. New snow lay unbroken as far as he could see. The trail leading from his cabin was buried deep. He longed to light his fire. Instead, he put on his heavy wool trousers and jacket, climbed up the wide window sill and pulled down the end of a long stick strung with a few remaining hard, flat loaves of bread, each with a hole in it. He slid off a loaf, broke it up and stuffed his pockets. He pulled on his stiff boots and wound the leather thongs around his legs to close the boots to the snow. He put on his thick bearskin parka and went out to strap on his skis.

He had been called upon to decree the fate of an abandoned baby boy found wrapped in a wolf skin. In winter, a foundling had to be set out to die if no one had the means to take it in. He did not like to judge that sort of thing, and his reluctance made it more difficult to break trail in the powdery snow. He had to lift the skis for each stride instead of gliding thoughtlessly, and the laden skis were as heavy as his thoughts.

A forest surrounded the tiny hand-hewn log cabin where the baby had been found. As Väinö brushed by the trees, heavy snow fell hard to the ground along his way. He put together the words that he had to say as he trudged in the cold: "Without parents, child, you cannot survive until spring."

Inside the cabin sat the old man. The bread-pole across the rafters over his head was empty. His fire was dead. Väinö did not look into the woven pinewood basket where he knew the baby lay. He declared his judgment and hurried to leave.

Then he stopped with his hand on the iron ring of the door pull. Slowly he turned back to the baby boy, leaned over the basket and took his tiny hand. "Yet I, Väinämöinen, have no child." He lifted the baby and looked into his bright eyes.

"I could sing to you and tell you stories."

He wrapped the baby carefully inside his great bear coat and strapped on his skis. Then he strode out into the winter cold, keeping the child next to his heart.

"Once there was a beautiful maiden of the air," he sang as he slid into stride on his own trail. "On her breeze floated the seeds of all the stories. . . ."

AFTERWORD

Väinämöinen stories are rooted in a prehistoric tradition of oral poetry sung by storysingers called *tietajat* or "knowers." The hero they sing of is not a warrior but a storysinger too. His power is in his song.

The stories were collected by Elias Lönnrot (1802-1884), a country doctor and classical scholar, who first came across the *runos* in his travels. He made twelve journeys to find storysingers—on foot, by horseback, on skis and by boat—as far north as the Arctic, as far south as Estonia and through parts of eastern Finland.

Lönnrot wove the stories together in his own way, as storysingers do, into the epic of the Finnish people, the *Kalevala*. When it was published, in 1835, and completed in 1849, it became an important focus of Finnish national identity.

Three recent English translations have made the *Kalevala* accessible to the present generation of storyteller, who will find room to play among the versions by Keith Bosley (Oxford University Press), Francis Magoun (Harvard University Press) and Eino Friberg (Otava, Helsinki).

In this book, the ancient stories pass through the heart of yet another storyteller.

The illustrations for this book are done in gouache and Derwent pencils on Arches watercolor paper. The snowy mist into which Väinämöinen disappears at the end (a more gentle departure than Lönnrot's choice) is done with ink and airbrush over gouache.

Finnish, a Finno-Ugrian language unrelated to English, is pronounced with the accent on the first syllable: *Ká-le-va-la*, *Väí-nä-möi-nen*. The ä is pronounced somewhat like the a in "that." The ö is pronounced like the e in "wet." Both vowels in the diphthongs are individually sounded, but blended a bit.

ACKNOWLEDGMENTS

Thanks to Harri Siitonen, Karen Meadows, Julie Hochstrasser, Laura McGee Kvasnosky and The Finnish American Home Association Library for information and guidance, and to my sons, Josh, Ben and Jerome, who enlivened this storytelling.

Particular thanks are due to Barbara Holdridge, my knowing and caring editor.

M.M.

Colophon

Designed by Barbara Holdridge
Text composed in Caslon 540 by Brushwood Graphics Inc.,
    Baltimore, Maryland
Display type composed in Neuland Solid and Neuland Inline
    by TypeOne, San Rafael, California
Printed on Japanese Matte Art paper and bound by
    Colorprint Offset, Hong Kong